RIGHT NOW: it's Time to HEAL

AF624629

Nashaya Mac

BookLeaf Publishing

Presentation by *BookLeaf Publishing*

Web: www.bookleafpub.com

E-mail: info@bookleafpub.com

ISBN: 9789357442664

First edition 2023

The first book was dedicated to the ones that encouraged me to keep going and this book is dedicated to

THERAPY.

We have all experienced trauma, it is necessary for growth. Right now, it is time to heal.

PREFACE

Pieces of poetry...
This cozy little lie I created in the image of perfection
So filled with abjection
I took a hammer to my reflection
Crack
Went those expectations that I seemed to fall short of
Any time I thought I was getting a leg up In this lie and learning to stand on my own But lies aren't set in stone so
They don't make a sturdy foundation
Crack
Went their dreams of my husband, our house, our kids.
I just wanted to live so I never accomplished this. I would build men up and leave them, knowing this lie was never enough,
I was never enough.
Crack
Went the desire to keep up with the Jones. Like whoever chose them, must not know that skeletons are like ruby slippers, They always bring you back home.
There's no place like home

Control

We say we want to heal from the past
But we hold onto all the weapons that hurt us
Vowing
To never let them prosper again
We group them together in clasped fists And
squeeze
Never letting go
Turning red fingers into pins and needles And
Removing circulation to the source
Clustering those traumas with force
So they can never hurt us again
Hold on
Until one slips
Out of our hand, stinging on its descent But
freeing up That space like sand
The weapons slowly begin to slip away
Gripping tighter so we never feel that way again
And choking
The life from
The things that once hurt us
Never realizing we continue to hurt us By
carrying Those tools daily, that hurt us
They will continue to hurt us
Let go!
Extinguishing their control.

Haikus: propaganda, not guilty, innocent, life

Search for black justice
Is on the agenda for
nobody, Just us

The verdict of one
The death of another, no
justice, just reset

Lips plant on my cheek
A kiss never felt so sweet
You've been waiting years

I met you in the
Messed up part of life, you're good
Now I can't get right

Dirt and Discomfort

There is no way to erase the pains of the past.
But we can fade the scars that bind us,
Plant new trees along the pathways to those
memories
White Magnolia petals floating in the breeze,
Pink gardenias adding color where it's bleak,
And climbing honeysuckles' sweet golden
nectar,
Blurring our taste buds with possibilities.

Adjoining these tragedies with objects of peace
Revisiting those moments comes with more ease
Realizing healing has begun where the thorns
Once replaced the trees
Becoming less focused on the prick but rather
seeking its beauty
The thorns are vital for the forest to grow.

Amongst the trees and the bush below
Beneath the shade of the canopy above
We learn, and love and heal
Until the day when the path is unkempt
And the traumas once contained
Now are the beauty of it.

The scars will fade and stories become less clear
Where healing has happened, will never disappear
Because the seeds were planted and the forest has shown
That there’s beauty even in tragedy, now it's time to move on

Chronos

Tomorrow isn't promised
but we waste today like
we've got time to spare.
Minutes slip away like
second chances we never take
like engagements we never make
like dreams we never share.

Time is the empty box we receive.
Gifted to us but wrapped in nothing
no glitter or technology to captivate our eyes
just a plain box so we cast it aside.
Filling it with objects that can wait
another day until it's too late
and only memories are there.

Glancing at the box as it disintegrates,
we scramble for objects of extinguishing desire
which we thought we could return and reignite
making a mess of our minds as
we scavenge for latent priorities
revisiting old hobbies and relishing memories
Subsequently losing more time.

Kairos

Flakes of silver and frozen fractals
Float over my dystopian paradise
A moment, encapsulated in time
Smiles plastered beneath empty eyes
Picturesque lies
A thousand words that weren't true

Joy sits on my mantle
Surrounded by glass and water
Protected from the elements
It looks happy there

Settling back into perfection
Until my world is shaken up again

Merryland

He challenged me to be more
Patient
Be more compassionate
Be more present
Be more silent

Be more resilient
Be more forgiving
Be more gentle

Be more caring
Be more affectionate
Be more understanding

Be more passenger
Be more follower
Be more listener

Be more giving
Be more living
Be more spontaneous

Be more shoulder
Be more hugger
Be more witness

Be more white dress
Be more confess
Be more wife

Be more supporter
Be more mother
Be more partner

Be more homemaker
Be more caretaker
Be more foundation

Be more build wealth
Be more good health
Be more mature

Be more love showed
Be more grow old
Be more adventure

He challenged me to be more Woman
So he can be more Man

Son of the Soil

I asked you to love me slowly
In lieu of sex, you helped me wash my hair
And cook dinner
And hang my pictures.
You acknowledged my fears of rejection
And eased my issues with trust.
Noting that you will answer every call if you
must
But you may not always be
Available to converse.
You understand my attention thirst
So you provide libations, within reason.
I don't want to just love you
Until next season, so you
Plant the herbs for our spice garden to grow.
Guiding my hands as we weed through my
insecurities
And dig holes for forgiveness to sow,
Pruning is necessary.
Second chances budding like perennials
Blooming under ripe conditions.
Patience is mandatory.
Nourishing our foundation
And hydrating our minds,
Love takes time.

I asked
What do you need from me
To make your love grow?
You replied, let me guide you,
As we till through your insecurities and
Plant your trust in me.
Let me confide in you
When I need a place of respite
And a listening ear.
Let me shelter you
From the winds of negativity
And the rays of doubt.
Let me take root beside you
So I can sprout with
The lover I find in you.
Everyday, just continue
To give me the chance to
Love you.

Apex

In the midnight hour of despair
We often see things that aren't fair
We pout our woes
And pick our nose
In hopes to find some gold in there

Six more weeks of winter

Birds chirp and the wing sings
These are the early signs of spring

Mosquitos awaken and torture my soul
These are the early signs of spring

Days grow longer, but night's still cold
These are the early signs of spring

Cars are packed for all four seasons
These are the early signs of spring

Watching the moon with no reason
These are the early signs of spring

Tiny critters and flowers that bloom
These are the early signs of spring

Saying good night to Winter's gloom
These are the early signs of Spring

Excavated Gems

When you left I could not breathe
I could not eat, I could not sleep
I thought nothing would come of me
As I lay there in my bed to weep

But then you gave me something more
A love story worth living for
You dried my eyes and wiped my tears
And told me living starts right here

Your tiny head upon my chest
In my dreams, I laid to rest
The biggest life I've ever known
With selfless love, my heart has grown

For now I write these songs to you
Of courage and of love so true

285

I am sitting in Atlanta Traffic watching all the cars go by until I switch lanes, hoping I will begin to curse as well. Suddenly coming to a screeching halt, the lane I was just in accelerates to racecar speeds and they're off. Watching the tail lights of the delivery truck that used to be in front of me disappear beyond the hill.
Pissed.
Now I am wondering why did I switch lanes in the first place? I should have just stayed where I was instead of presuming everyone else's race.
Annoyed.
This traffic is so unpredictable and every time I think the other lane is moving forward without me, my envy takes over and I switch lanes again. So worried about what they are doing that I fail to notice how far I have come. All I focused on was traffic zipping by without me, although my wheels were turning also.
Breathe.
Inhale.
Ease.
I slow my tempo to the beat of the road. No longer allowing envy and the need for speed to

control me. Ebbing with the freeway, as traffic loosens up and flows past the invisible backup. Focus.

Keeping my eyes fixed ahead of me, I see those familiar tail lights gleaming. FedEx 652-118z is beside me. Now I'm passing. Smiling because I didn't allow Atlanta traffic to get the best of me. Learning to stay in my lane, remain calm, and let the cars be. I will end up exactly where I need to be. Patience, my exit is coming.

Trenta

I saw it sitting there. Poised on the top of my head like it was finally home. Reclaiming my done, it conveyed ownership. A message of which I hadn't quite gotten the grip. It was noticeable like a streak of bad luck. I wanted it GONE. But it was reluctant. And I knew I couldn't pluck it because it would only spread like Ivy. Growing back in couplets so I went with it. Dressing it up with wise quotes. Smoothing the lines my brows wrote. I named it Younge. Proclaiming 30 was the age of wisdom. It sat there. Atop my head. A single gray hair.

Witcho Robinson Self

I've always been told I was too good to be true
What if too much for them was just enough for you?What if the reason you wanted multiples is because they didn't add up to me?
And the beauty that you seek is the very thing I hide in me?
What if I were your missing piece and instead of picking me back up
You tried to mold them to the shape of me?
But they were too smooth for my rugged edges and too commercial for my dimpled curves.
You wanted unorthodox wrapped in a bright orange box with a purple sequin bow on top, with blue polka dots.
Instead you got Cream pops, and dream pops, and cute little pink ones with strawberries on top
But no polka dots.
You didn't have me.

Night Cap

Candles crackle as sultry tunes play
Dancing in the shadows amongst the beat
Long hair spread effortlessly
Across the fibers of the sheets
Eyes closed in hypnotic anticipation
Of a longing lover's kiss
Embraced with much hesitation
Placed on the forehead not the lips

Affirmation of Healing

I am present, not focusing on the past or worrying about the future. I am here, in this space, mindful of my thoughts and actions. I understand my past was a lesson and carry those teachings with me. I will not allow them to dictate my future. I am the controller of my destiny. I am conscious of what thoughts I hold onto and what thoughts I allow to pass through me. I act in accordance with what is best for me. I am the keeper of my decisions and my consequences. I will not allow others to impose their will upon me. If it does not align, it will pass through me. I understand that everything is moving around me. I am healed and constantly healing.

Pursuit

This little part, is called happiness
Stop measuring your reflection against a filter
It is designed to only expose the best of you
Disregard the rest of you
Because nobody likes you when you aren't perfect
When your clothes no longer fit
When your hair doesn't flip or lay
How it's supposed to
But who told you that your flaws
Were in need of correction?
Following social media directions
Like it's the latest dance craze
Not recognizing the error in your ways
You are beautiful and your
Happiness should project that
Stop holding onto the fact that
He doesn't like you, she is a size two
That shit wasn't meant for YOU!
Your figure is full of love and life
Experiences
No need to try to cover this
Because it's as good as it gets.
Accept who you are and
Dance in your underwear!

No matter the stops or stares
You deserve to be there.
You have survived so much
And have the scars to map your strength
Directing you to love and inner peace
Rejuvenation and energy
You are ascending to your peak!
That sigh of relief
That favorite warm drink
That cozy pillow and cool sheet
That smile
That stride
That returning confidence
That right there,
Is called happiness

Marie Sherlock

Bend me over
No need for foreplay
I've been ready since you hit the doorway
Texting me all day
About what you gone do to this pussy
How you wanted to feel all this gushy
Around your shaft
Plunging deep while you're smacking my ass
And pulling my hair
Taking me there
Time after time as you go deeper
Making my knees weaker
Forgetting all the ways I can't keep ya
Tonight, I'm your keeper.

Keeping your secrets nestled between my thighs
You tell me everything you try to hide
Professing your ambitions on this clit
You said cum for me, so I did
And you ate it
Slurping my mango juices
Insatiable, you want more of it
And I oblige
Weaving my fingers in your locs
As I prepare for this ride.
Baby, dive.

Only coming up for air
You stay there
And play there
And soak these sheets like we ain't got to lay there

And yes, it's sweet
As I kiss your succulent lips
Dripping the essence of me
You press your full erection into me
Sliding in so effortlessly
There's no need to breathe
No need to speak
Nothing in this world but you and me
Gazing
Passionately
Miraculously
We forgot the world existed
Outside of you and me

But then your phone rings
And reality sets in
You dismount my body
As your phone displays
BAE is calling

Christmas Caroll

I am TIRED of being alone
Tried of having no one on my phone
Tired of simply coming home
To me again
I am tired of starting over too
Reintroducing myself like
"Hi I'm Nashaya, how are you?"
In my mind hoping that you're looking for
Something of value
Not just legs you can spread in two

I am tired of being the single friend
Every event introducing them to a new man
Because the one from last time, ain't here again
And everyone is looking like who is he
Or just sending in a solo RSVP because
Those stares are just as fun
And they seat me at the table with the other solo ones
Hoping I'd hit it off with her grade school best friend

I am tired of Hallmark movies telling me love
Is on the other end of heartache
Or healing is better in a small town at a

Tiny cafe where the barista knows my name
And has been waiting for me.
He's actually educated, successful, wealthy and sexy
Ready to sweep me off my feet

I'm tired of Christmas in my 30s with no husband no kids and no tree
It's just my bunnies, my mother, and me so there's no need for festivities
I am tired of being single past thirty
Where every qualifying black man is into polygamy And I'm somehow revered like
I have three eyes because I don't want a sister wife
No! I don't want to share at all
Do you think I've worked this hard and waited this long
To schedule sex or share you with her?
Shit, I don't even like women!

I am tired of black men thinking
They can't find refuge in black women
Like they have to hide their scars
As if we can't already see them
Baby, I just need you to talk to me.
Open up to me.
Tell me the stories of your healing
Let me place your hands on your wounds

And breathe life into them.

I am so FUCKING tired of being alone
Not to be mistaken that I don't love me
Because I am the mutha fucking shit
But I don't accept just anything
I require more
I desire more
I deserve everything that I bring to him
And more!

I am just so fucking tired of being Miss
Independent
Acting like I don't need a man for shit
Like I don't want to be submissive and
Ride his dick
I want all of it!
I don't want to pay all my bills
Or have to deal with all the world's ails
Go on only girls' trips
Wishing for baecations but making the best of it
Because damn it I'm going to make the best of it.
I just don't want to do this by myself
I want to come home to you

Shay's Prayer

I want an authentic love. A love I don't have to close my eyes to feel. Building organically on basic conversations. Not forced communication because we look good together. I want to pace around the house finding random stuff to get into because I'm too engaged in this conversation with you to do anything else. Like drawing circles around all the dots on my leopard print sheets, but I don't have leopard print sheets! or racing the drops of rain on the windowpane. I want to accidentally fall in love with you, while dozing off at 3 am or star gazing on some unnamed dirt road. We could call it Agape. My perfect gentleman that embraced the lady in me when she didn't even think she could be seen. Not as his "Enlightened Queen" but as his life partner and peace. I want to be his confidant and his place of relief. He will be my all-inclusive mountain retreat. Planning for this vacation is never easy but it's always worth it in the end. I want him to plan a life with me. Protect the wife in me. I can take the arguments and even some sleepless nights, as long as we maintain our commitment to our partnership and the willingness to get it right. I want a love I can heal with. Someone that understands that love requires nurturing and room. We can create this safe space, where tears are a part of our love language, and we heal with words of affirmation and physical touch. Giving and receiving the gifts of unconditional positive regard. We embody these acts of service as a right; not a chore. Present in each moment, we won't notice how our physical appeal may change. Still beautiful in my eyes because your soul remains the same. I want someone to love me even on my funky days. Love me through my stubborn ways. Love me day and night the same. I just want to love again. Like an old R&B jazz song or a holiday Hallmark movie. I want us to be that cheesy. Make the kids cover their eyes because mommy and daddy are kissing again. I want to love you out loud. To dance to our favorite song in the grocery store aisle and in the moon light. A love that doesn't let me sleep at night. I deserve an ugly love, a beautiful love, an unrelenting get-on-my-nerves just because it's love. A love that still wants to take me on dates. Or one that stays up and waits when my life runs late. I want that "nah, my wife is crazy" love when anyone approaches him with foolishness that doesn't align with us. We deserve a love that is the first and last thought of the day. I need a love that aligns with our spiritual identity; you, me and our divinity. A childish love that grows to infinity and beyond. That family bond. I will be my lover's best friend. The one that pushes him and speaks up for his best interest.

I want to grow old with this love. Someone I can spent the majority of my life with, making me forget how the primary of my life went without him. I want a love that makes waiting make sense. One that truly shows me those learned lessons were preparing us for this. Someone that knows that I will cry to Disney movies and won't judge me for it. Just hold me.

I deserve a love that's ready. Not emotionally unavailable or still exploring women outside of me. I want the good parts of that old-fashioned love, not 15 years later staying just for the children. He stays because he loves me. And prays because he loves me.

I deserve this kind of love. He deserves this kind of love for me. I am growing impatient and starting not to believe but somewhere inside, I'm holding on to the hope that he'll find me. In enough time to reignite this positive belief. So to you, wherever you are, understand you will have to overcome the initial skepticism of my heart but I am here.

For now. With love.
          We'll see.
I love you.

John Henry

My family relies on me
To carry the hammer that breaks
Every generational curse
From changing my last name
To not having an illegitimate birth
To getting an education
And making something of myself
Creating successes in my career
And building generational wealth

But they forget the part about being happy
Creating a space for your mind to find peace
And your thoughts to find sleep
Or your eyes not to weep
Because this hammer is so fucking heavy
And everyone is watching me
Waiting for me to mess up,

I mean succeed

Just so they can pass judgement on me
Like "I told you she couldn't do it"
"She wouldn't go any further than me"
Because then they wouldn't be
Only failures in the family

My family tugs at my roots
With a fine tooth comb to these kinks
And curls of culture
Reminding me that it's just
Pretty words for Nappy
Fancy ways to make me happy
When my spirals assimilate to get that job
Or when my vernacular changes while
addressing
The mob of nonmelanated onlookers
Also judging me
For reasons just because they see
Legacy
Building

I am under construction and this
Hammer is so fucking heavy
Swing
I want to drop it
Swing
I want to quit
Swing
I want to walk away and say fuck it
But I just can't pry my hands from its grip
So I keep swinging

I raise my tired arms and condition my hair

Soothing each strand that frizzes and gets out of line
I raise my tired hands to stop my family
Leaving them to wade in their negativity alone
I raise one leg at a time and stamp new
Footprints into this proverbial family sand
I turn my tired back to them, not in abandonment
But as a beacon that says follow me

I swing this hammer again and again
Sometimes reluctantly
But I can't give up on me
And I won't give up again
So I raise these tired arms one more time
And swing
My way into happy,
Just swing

The Resurrection of the Little Black Girl

I can face you now.
I can look in the mirror and declare that I am proud
Of who you are growing up to be
I see your smile through your eyes and understand that there's no easy street
I catch the rhythm of your stride as you dance to your own beat
Little brown girl
I see you glowing
I see your magic flowing
I see you manifesting all the things you held on to
And I see you letting go
Forgiving yourself for the times you didn't show up for you
Allowing yourself to breathe again
Allowing yourself to believe again

Little brown girl
I taste your struggle, the one that you try to hide under your coat sleeves
I taste their attempt at your defeat
I taste the strength of your divinity

I taste your passion and your energy
I taste your victory

Little brown girl
I hear you
I hear them laughing when someone can't
enunciate your powerful name
I hear your mama calling from the house
because you can't play that game
I hear you whispering on the phone knowing it's
way past curfew
I hear you encouraging yourself when no one
else believed in you

Little brown girl
I feel you
I feel your heart skip a beat when you're in
father's embrace
I feel the expectations of your family that gave
you that face
I feel the knot in your throat when you take that
stage
I feel your joy. I feel your relief.

Little brown girl
I see you
I see your kinky hair and luscious lips
I see your high cheekbones and defined hips
I see your thick eyebrows and sun-toasted skin

I see your pronounced nose and pearly grin

Little brown girl
I smell the burn of that hot comb, they used to try and tame your kinks and curls
I smell your Queen Helen, Blue Magic, and your essential oils
I smell your attitude with no hesitation because brown girl "say that shit"
I smell their attempt at disrespect because they just don't get it.
I smell your deliverance

Little Brown girl
I see and hear you.
Little brown girl
I embody and feel you.
Little brown girl
I am here for you.
Little brown girl
I am you and you live within me too.
Little brown girl
This is just a reminder that
I love you

www.ingramcontent.com/pod-product-compliance
Lightning Source LLC
Chambersburg PA
CBHW051746130826
49812CB00033B/1026
9789357442664